The Rock of Ages at the Taj Mahal

Unquiet Meditations by
Meg Barnhouse

Skinner House Books
Boston

Published by Skinner House Books, an imprint of the Unitarian Universalist Association, 25 Beacon Street, Boston, Massachusetts 02108-2800.

Printed in the USA.

ISBN 1-55896-377-4

10 9 8 7 6 5 4 3 2 1
02 01 00 99

Thank you Pat, for getting me started writing these pieces.

Thank you Kim, for your wisdom, your love, and your fire.

Thanks to the writers at The Center of the Universe, to the Unitarian Universalist Church of Spartanburg, to my funny and handsome sons, and thank you Group, my oldest friends.

Contents

All Will Be Well

All will be well, and all will be well, and all manner of things will be well." This is one of the mantras used in the Christian meditation tradition. Don't think it comes from a dewy-eyed Pollyanna. The woman to whom it is credited, Dame Julian of Norwich, is the same one who, when her mule got stuck on a mountain road in a rainstorm, dismounted, shook her fist at the sky, and shouted, "God! If this is how you treat your friends, it's no wonder you don't have many!"

Lately I have been experimenting with repeating, "All will be well, and all will be well, and all manner of things will be well." I try it out in different situations. Sometimes I feel stupid affirming that all will be well. What about things that aren't well and don't look like they're ever going to be well? It's hard to see the whole picture from where I stand at this moment in my life.

There is a story of a Chinese farmer who had a fine horse show up in his pasture one day. "How marvelous!" all the neighbors said. "Maybe," said the farmer. His son tried to ride the horse and the horse threw him, breaking the son's leg. "How awful," said the neighbors. "Maybe," replied the farmer. Then the Emperor's army came through town to draft young men for war. The farmer's son was spared because of his broken leg.

I can't tell, in the grand scheme of life, whether things are turning out well or not. To affirm that "all will be well, and all will be well, and all manner of things will be well" is difficult for me. There are child abusers and torturers and AIDS and oil spills and a multitude of other horrors in this world.

Here is what I do know. I know that I have a choice between hope or despair when viewing the world and my future. Each choice has equal evidence in its favor. Each is affirmed and underscored by my life experience. How do I decide between them? I choose the one that brings the most joy, the most healing, the most compassion to my life and to the world. In despair I'm no good to anyone. I stop functioning well, I drag through the days, I deal with horrors that haven't even happened yet. I don't enjoy my children, food, sex, or any of the other dazzling pleasures of my life.

When my mother was dying of cancer, she said to me, "Meggie, everything that happens to me is good." That was a statement of her faith. I was a cynical twenty-three-year-old seminary student. My mother's faith sounded naive and silly. I was in despair over her suffering, but she was not in despair, and it was her suffering. Suddenly, it seemed presumptuous to despair over her suffering when she was choosing not to.

As I experiment with this mantra and risk feeling stupid, which is a feeling I despise, I ask myself, "Which is more stupid: to despair my whole life just in case things aren't going to end well, or to live in joy and hope my whole life, whether or not things turn out well?" I'm going to keep singing this mantra to my fears. All will be well, and all will be well, and all manner of things will be well.

Fruit of Like Kind

One summer I was working at the Walter Reed Army Hospital, learning how to be a chaplain. I was twenty-two years old, and I didn't know what I was doing. But Walter Reed is a teaching hospital, and the patients there were kind enough to let me practice on them. I worked a women's cancer ward and a men's neurosurgery ward for three months in the summer of 1978. The hospital gave me a white jacket to wear with the word "Chaplain" embroidered in blue on the pocket. I asked my supervisor what a chaplain did. He said, "You're a chaplain. Whatever you do is what a chaplain does." Every afternoon five of us trainees would meet to talk about what we had done that morning in our wards.

I got an education that summer about how people react to ministers. When I walked into one lady's room, she started screaming, "Oh my God, I'm going to die! I'm going to die!" She thought the doctors had sent me in to prepare her for the bad news. I stood rooted to the spot, totally blank about what to do. The nurses hustled me out of her room and soothed her.

My supervisor asked me, "What did you learn from that?" I thought, next time I should say something like, "Hello, I'm making rounds this morning and I thought I'd stop in." That seemed better than, "Hello, I'm the chaplain and you're not going to die."

Once I was sitting with an older man, an officer, who was waking up from anesthesia. He was lying on his stomach with his face turned toward me. His eyes fluttered open, and I said, "Hi, I'm Meg, the chaplain, and I'm just sitting with you while you wake up."

"Why are you doing this?" he asked, groggy with the medication.

"This? It's my job, I'm the chaplain, and I'm just sitting with you while . . ."

"NO, no, no, you don't understand. Why are you doing this?"

"Doing this . . . what?"

He was getting frustrated now. "Minister. Chaplain." He was struggling. "Why are you doing this?"

"Well, I felt like God called me to be a minister . . ."

"No, no, no, no," I still wasn't answering the question that was burning in his brain. "You're pretty enough. Why aren't you married and bearing fruit of like kind?" With that he went back to sleep.

I think he was asking me why wasn't I getting married and having children instead of being a hospital chaplain.

Some people think ministers talk a different language that is straight out of the King James Bible. There's a story about a little girl who dashes into the living room holding a big dead rat by the tail. She doesn't see that the minister is visiting, and that he and the parents are making polite conversation. She says, "Mom! Dad! Look!! I found this rat down in the barn and I hit him with the shovel and I hit him again and then I took him by the tail and I bashed him against the wall and then I bashed him again . . ." Then she notices the minister sitting there. "And then the dear Lord took the little fella ho-o-o-ome."

People act a little strange when they find out you're a therapist, too. They can't help watching what they say for signs of insanity, but they don't really need to worry. The therapists I know, myself included, are just as weird as most normal people.

I am surprised and grateful, as a minister and a therapist, that people talk to me at all, what with the temptation to speak in King James English and having to guard against sounding insane. To those of you who speak when you see me: thank you. And now, verily I must forthwith depart and prepare a repast for my kindred.

Demons, Dobermans and Naked Pentecostals

One summer I saw an ad in the paper for a tent revival. It was going to be a deliverance service. For those unfamiliar with the lingo, that's a service where the preacher tries to cast demons out of people. The little community where the service was to be held had the reputation of being a rough place.

I was working as a college chaplain at the time, and when I told my friends at the faculty lunch table that I was planning to go to the deliverance service, they begged me not to go alone. Dr. Mann, a friend who taught Old Testament courses, agreed to come with me. I promised him there would be plenty of people and no one would notice us at all.

On the night of the revival, we found the tent in a pasture by the railroad tracks. Parked in the pasture was an old school bus, faded red, with the words "Preacher Bob, Statesville, NC" painted on the side in powder blue letters. Preacher Bob, his wife, and their two daughters were there, each of whom weighed at least three hundred pounds. They had a huge black Doberman, who bounded up to our car and sniffed at us intimately as we walked to the tent. I assured my friend that plenty more people would be coming soon. We took our seats, trying to look inconspicuous.

I was worried that the preacher would come yell at us—something about "those who came to scoff and stayed to pray," but he didn't. We hadn't really come to scoff, but I wasn't sure how he would feel about our coming because my hobby is collecting odd religious experiences.

Seven more people came. It was a challenge to get lost in that crowd. As the service started, Dr. Mann, chewing nervously on his unlit pipe, leaned over to me and said, "Meg, if I have to get a demon cast out of me I—am—going—to—kill—you." We tried to blend in, but we weren't sure how to look Pentecostal. I said "Amen" a couple of times, and we sang loudly when it was time to sing. The two daughters stood up and sang "Suppertime in Heaven." It made me hungry.

The casting out of demons went fine, as far as I could tell. Women shrieked and fell down unconscious and there was some writhing and jerking. Everyone seemed to feel better when it was done. The people were gracious and they didn't make Dr. Mann or me feel like geeks or sinners for not coming up to have demons cast out, even though every other person there did, except the preacher's family. And the Doberman.

The experience was satisfyingly odd. I am growing less and less clear these days on what is an odd form of religion and what is not. I know lots of people who view my own brand of Unitarian Universalist Pagan-ish Christian-ish spirituality as odd. I think I feel a kinship with people on religion's wild side.

I crave passion in my own spiritual life, and I am drawn to the passion of folks on the fringe. I admire their willingness to look foolish. Take the twenty naked Pentecostals packed into one Trans-Am I heard about on the news. They were picked up by police for weaving down a Louisiana highway. They heard God tell them he was going to destroy the wicked rural Texas town where they were living. He wanted them to sell everything and put their trust only in him. They started out clothed and in several cars, but somehow their call to radical trust led to them being all in one car and naked in Louisiana. I know the story is crazy, but it is wonderful as well. Those people were throwing themselves into their religion—like the people writhing and falling down in the tent in that pasture by the railroad tracks; like me, when I have drumming and a bonfire. I wish more of that for all of us.

Waitressing in the Sacred Kitchens

I love for a waitress to call me "Hon." It's comforting. She doesn't know me and I don't know her, but we fit into well-worn, ancient categories: I am the Hungry One and she is the One Who Brings Nourishment From the Unseen Source.

When I was younger, I worked as a waitress in Philadelphia and New Jersey. I learned useful things while serving food to strangers. I know how to rush around with my hands full, thinking about six things at the same time, which has stood me in good stead as the working mother of two small sons. I know that people are not at their best when they're hungry. That knowledge helps me to understand world events. If the citizens of the world were well fed, we'd have fewer wars and less mayhem.

The most helpful thing I grasped while waitressing was that some tables are my responsibility and some are not. A waitress gets overwhelmed if she has too many tables, and no one gets good service. In my life, I have certain things to take care of: my children, my relationships, my work, myself, and one or two causes. That's it. Other things are not my table. I would go nuts if I tried to take care of everyone, if I tried to make everybody do the right thing. If I went through my life without ever learning to say, "Sorry, that's not my table, Hon," I would burn out and be no good to anybody. I need to have a surly waitress inside myself that I can call on when it seems everyone in the world is waving an empty coffee cup in my direction. My Inner Waitress looks over at them, keeping her six plates balanced and her feet moving, and says, "Sorry, Hon, not my table."

One of the hardest lessons for me is learning how to blend my individuality with my role. I'm still learning this as a minister and as a therapist. I need a certain spiritual strength and a lessening of ego before I can take on a role and let people relate to me in my function as a therapist or a minister rather than as a fascinating woman with a birthday, a favorite color, a song I can sing better than it is on the album, and cool stories of travels to foreign lands. It's not easy to lose myself that way and I'm still not good at it.

When I was in seminary, all of us were struggling with how to blend and balance our individuality within the role of minister. We found that most people have a strong idea of how a minister should look and talk and behave. I can join a new group of people, talking and laughing, being normal, and the moment they find out I'm a minister the laughter dies as they check back over the things they've said in front of me, trying to remember if they've sworn or sinned or said something politically incorrect. It's hard. It makes some of us want to lie about what we do. It makes some ministers want to moon the group. That would banish those burdensome expectations.

There are times, though, when people need help to draw strength and comfort from the Spirit. As a minister, I'm the one who is there at the hospital or the funeral home. I'm the one who is there in my office when the family comes hoping for peace and clarity.

It is my job to bring nourishment to hungry souls from the sacred kitchens where the Spirit cooks up healing and comfort. It doesn't really matter at that moment when my birthday is, or that purple is my favorite color. What matters is the function I perform when I stand in the broad stream of history and symbol, faith and mythology, and let something larger than myself work through me, through the role I'm filling. What matters is that I'm smelling the rich aromas of hope and joy rising from the dishes I hold in my arms, and I know what it means to the people who need it.

Come sit down, Hon. Are you hungry?

Laundromat Outlaw

I broke the rules at the laundromat. I plead ignorance. For most of my life I have been rich and I didn't know it. I have lived with a washer and dryer right in the same house with me. My new house didn't have either appliance, so for the first week I took my clothes to the Clean 1 Washeteria.

It looks the same as the laundromat I used at school in New Jersey. It looks the same as the one I used to go to with my mother when I was nine in Statesville, North Carolina. There are rows of washing machines, rows of dryers, a woman supervising the room, and a blaring TV. People sit on plastic chairs reading or watching soap operas while their laundry washes and dries.

I have a problem with sitting. I'm recently divorced and still in that attention-deficit stage where I can't focus on anything for longer than fifteen minutes. I could no more sit and watch TV while my clothes washed than climb Mount Everest.

I put my clothes in their washers and left. When I got back the clothes were done. I had been gone so long I was surprised my clothes were still in the washers. I expected them to be in wet heaps on one of the counters. I put everything in two dryers and left again. When I got back after a couple of hours, the supervisor was waiting for me, leaning on her mop and looking stern. She said my clothes had been sitting in those dryers for an hour and people were waiting to use the machines and I really should be more consistent. (I think she meant "considerate.") I was horrified. I am never inconsiderate. Well, only when I'm driving. When not under the influence of asphalt, I'm a wonderful person.

If someone needed the dryer and my clothes were finished, why didn't they just take my clothes out and leave them piled on a counter? The laundromat I remember in New Jersey had piles of wet clothes on the counters, piles of dry clothes in rolling baskets. No one had to sit around stewing because somebody's clothes were finished and they weren't back to get them. The clothes would have been wrinkled, but wrinkles were the price you paid for freedom. The culture of this laundromat is different. The women sat, needing to do their wash, not willing to move my clothes. And I had to stand there and be scolded by the laundry lady.

I hate being scolded. It takes me back to third grade, and that was not a good year. I stuffed my dry clothes in bags and slunk away, a laundromat outlaw. I hate breaking rules by accident, so I conducted a completely unscientific poll on the Law of the Laundromat. I asked a number of people to pretend someone else's wash was finished and sitting in the machine. Would they take out the wash and leave the person's wet clothes on the counter? Would they take dry clothes out of a dryer and leave them in one of those rolling wire baskets? At first the responses were divided along the Mason-Dixon line, with Southerners represented by my best friend, who says you don't mess with other people's messes.

Another Southern friend said nonsense, she'd have taken my clothes out and dumped them on the counter in a skinny minute if she needed the machine. She is a first-grade teacher, and they know how to take charge of an unruly world.

Maybe it's politeness that kept those women waiting for the machines occupied by my laundry. Maybe it was passivity. I can't tell. Sometimes politeness and passivity look the same to me. I would prefer not to stomp around stewing, waiting for other people to do what I think is the right thing. I don't want them to stomp around waiting for me to do what they think is the right thing, either. They would probably have a long wait.

I am going to try to figure out what the right thing is at this laundromat before I go back. That supervisor lady is someone I don't want to cross again. Meanwhile, these days I have a washer and dryer at my house. I'm going to go kiss them now.

Be There

I know beauty and grace are all around me. Sometimes I know how to be there for it. Other times I get distracted by my bank balance dipping into the negative, by my child coughing, by my body aging, or by someone somewhere being disappointed in me.

Usually it is clear to me that I have the choice to stew about things or to be there for my life. In her book *The Intuitive Body*, Aikido Master Wendy Palmer writes that you get what you pay for when it comes to your attention. Whatever you pay attention to, that is what you get. If you pay attention to the things that are nuisances, your life feels like one big nuisance. If you pay attention to beauty and joy, then your life fills up with beauty and joy.

Last weekend I was paying attention to ninety-degree heat and shoving crowds, standing in line for the bumper car ride with my two boys. One of them kept changing his mind about the ride. What he really wanted to do was toss rubber chickens into a small pot, five tries for two dollars. My brain was a rubber chicken.

I had just dragged the children all over the fair, looking for the writers with whom I was supposed to sign books. I was also looking for the folks from my congregation who were selling beer. I couldn't find either group and the whole time I was looking, both boys were pulling on me and asking,

"Can we ride the rides now?" I didn't even have the energy to start the "do you know the difference between 'can' and 'may'?" discussion since my nine year old last time said, "Yeah, mom. 'May' is a month and 'can' is a tin container." Sigh. So I said, "Let's go ride the rides," and here we were in line and into my head came this thought: "I am in hell."

Once I saw my older son dive into a car and start twirling the wheel, waiting for the ride to start, I moved into the shade with his brother to watch. There my brain cooled off enough to remember to enjoy my life, to be there for the beauty and grace in that situation. I saw my son's mouth open wide with joy, its inside stained red by a tiger's blood-flavored shaved ice.

He was in bliss, being slammed from behind and from all sides by other bumper car drivers. He threw back his head and laughed, putting the pedal to the metal in reverse, snapping his head forward as he took aim and slammed into another car, looking sideways at the other driver, grinning, not quite able to believe this was actually allowed.

Jubilee. Bubbles of joy changed my breathing. I was having fun. Here was beauty and here was grace and here I was in the middle of it. Jubilee indeed.

County Fair

*S*he said, "I *never* take my children to the county fair."

"Why don't you?" I asked. I try to stay calm with people like this. I do understand how one should protect children from certain experiences at too young an age, but this woman had on a denim jumper with a big white collar and gold shoes and a bow in her hair the size of a roasting pan.

"Because of the things they see there!" she cried.

I'm trying to see what she means, and I think I know what it is. The freak shows are back. In the eighties, you didn't see the freaks and geek shows at the fair, but the snake girl has returned. "She has no bones in her entire body!" the marquee screams, "Yet she is alive and she will talk to you and answer any question you ask!" My boys said the thought of going into the snake girl's trailer gave them the creeps. Then they felt sorry for her, but that still didn't make them want to see her.

"At least she's making a living," I said. "People were going to be staring at her her whole life anyway, they may as well pay her to do it."

On the side of the next trailer, a picture of a woman's corpse was painted in garish colors. Blood dripped from her severed neck. The words read: "Beheaded supermodel's body kept alive for seven years!" I wanted to cover my children's eyes with my hand. They don't let me do that much anymore. We all said, "Eeeeuuuwwww!" and kept walking.

I'm guessing those are the kinds of things the lady didn't want her children to see. I don't blame her. Everybody has different ideas on how much to protect children. I'm going to tell you what I wish my children hadn't seen. It was the crowd of adults gawking at the goat who could blow up balloons. A clown was leading the goat around the fairgrounds. He wore gloves and carried balloons in the pocket of his yellow clown pants.

Now and then the clown and the goat would stop. The clown would pull out a balloon and clamp it with both hands under the goat's chin. The balloon would inflate with five or six steady puffs. Oooooh! said the kids. How cute. Aaaahhhhh, said the adults, amazed. That's the freak show I wanted to protect my children from seeing—the sight of adults standing slack-jawed, believing that nanny goat was blowing up balloons.

I would like my children to respect grown-ups. I would like them to see adults using their brains. "Watch the sides of the goat move in and out as it breathes," I told my boys. The goat was breathing shallow and fast. Her sides were rising and falling quickly at the same time that deep, slow puffs of air were inflating the balloons. The light dawned in my children's eyes.

"I bet he has a tube inside his gloves and the air comes from his sleeves!" said my ten year old.

"I bet he's blowing through an invisible tube he hides in his head!" said my seven year old.

I told them I'd put my money on the tube in the glove. There is a lot to be said for an education and some life experience. It helps to know ahead of time that goats don't blow up balloons. Once you're clear on that, you can make yourself notice what is happening in front of your eyes. It helps to know ahead of time that businesses don't make deals that lose them money; that governments go to war over money, not principles; that no one can really bend a spoon with their mind alone; that ministers aren't better people than anyone else; that just being rich doesn't make you interesting; that no one's breasts have ever gotten permanently bigger using one of the devices advertised in the backs of magazines; and that the only good way to lose weight is to eat less and exercise more. It helps to know these things so you can notice what really happens in front of your eyes, no matter how hard you wish something else were true.

I hate the fact that my kids saw grown-ups being duped. Oh, well. Better break it to them gently that we all stare slack-jawed sometimes, wanting something impossible to be true. I know I do, and they are going to catch me at it sometime soon.

A Life Well Spent

One night I heard an old man say, "I had a wasted life." I began wondering what it would take for me to say I had wasted my life. I could have lived a life where I only watched TV and cleaned my house. Then I would lie on my death bed and remember my life while wailing and gnashing my teeth in that clean, clean house. I could have been a company woman making six figures and working 60 hours a week, too busy for my family, my church, my garden, and taking small comfort in remembering that I had never missed a day of work.

As I lie on my death bed, what do I want to remember? Right now my relationship with my father is painful. I asked him four or five years ago to stop quoting the Bible to me because it made me feel like throwing up and screaming. He stopped immediately, even though the Bible is his reference, his rule, and his delight. We continue to talk every two or three months, but he has less and less to say. I don't know what I want to do about it. Part of me wants to give up. It would be a relief to surround myself only with people who are like-minded.

I don't want to remember being cut off from my father because he doesn't talk to me the way I would like him to talk to me. I don't want to look back on drifting away from my family because they are devoted Christians and I am Christian in ethics and Pagan in practice.

In *The Wheel of Life*, people told Elizabeth Kubler-Ross that when they went toward the Light, they were shown how all our lives are intertwined. Our actions and thoughts affect the Universe like ripples in a pond. People reported hearing the question: "What service have you rendered?" The Light asked them to consider whether they had made the highest and best choices in life, and whether they had learned the ultimate lesson of unconditional love.

I wish I hadn't read that passage. I'm not great at unconditional love. I try, but lots of people annoy me. Even when I have the time, attention, and patience to love unconditionally, I'm not sure what it involves. I know it doesn't mean being sweet and dewey-eyed and telling people they are wonderful no matter what. I know unconditional love involves disagreement and challenge. So how do I know, in each situation, what unconditional love involves?

What would be a life well spent for a regular, somewhat irresponsible, but often charming person without a lot of moral fortitude like myself? I heard one woman say she just wanted to live long enough to grow every kind of tulip there was. Another friend said she wanted to live long enough to see her daughter struggle with a seventeen-year-old daughter just like her.

What would satisfy me? I will be glad if I have raised my children with honesty and love; if I have made music with other people; if I have seen beauty and loved it; if I have learned how to get along with my relatives; if I have made a soul connection with Spirit, friends, and lovers; and if I have claimed my right to tell the truth as I see it. Oh, and I want to be wonderful. That's all.

Honey, They're Catholics

You couldn't really call my childhood church fundamentalist; we just had strong ideas about how things should be done. It was a conservative Scotch-Irish denomination called the Associate Reformed Presbyterian Church. We sang psalms instead of hymns, because hymns weren't from the Bible, therefore they were not divinely inspired.

We weren't supposed to call the first day of the week "Sunday." We called it "Sabbath." On Sabbath, we were not allowed to do anything but go to Sabbath school in the morning, followed by church, with church again in the evening. We could eat, nap, or memorize Bible verses during the times when we weren't at church. There was to be no bike riding, swimming, listening to music, or going out with friends. We ate a lot, napped a lot, and memorized tons of Bible verses.

All this was meant to make us spiritual. What it did was make us legalistic. We were great at following the letter of the law. We could set the alarm for midnight Sunday, and at 12:01, we'd play records and dance for a minute before tumbling back into bed. We found loopholes. We discovered that if you change your terminology, you can get by with more.

On our way to church, when we saw children on bicycles or headed to the lake with towels and rafts piled in the back of their parents' station wagons, we would whine, "Mama, *those* children get to ride bikes on Sabbath, and *those* children get to go to the lake." My mother would say, "Honey, they're Catholics."

I wanted to be a Catholic when I grew up. There was something definitely exotic about them. One of my aunts married one, and the whole family, when discussing her situation, would whisper, "Well, you know, she married a *Catholic*."

This called for more research. The conversation I remember best was one I had with my cousin Rebecca in the bushes beside her daddy's horse pasture. I had white shoe polish dabbed all over a poison ivy rash, which my mother said worked the same as calamine lotion.

"They have these big wafers they have to eat," Rebecca said, her eyes large and her voice portentous, "and the worse they've acted that week the worse those wafers taste." That didn't sound good. If that were true, those kids deserved to swim on Sabbath. Then again, that portentous tone of voice was the same one Rebecca used when she told me, "If you sit under a plum tree, and it's the full moon, and you lick a frog—you'll die."

Rebecca was my hero. One day when her older brothers had been teasing her beyond bearing, she went into the house and got their bug collection from their room. She made some chocolate chip cookie dough, ground up all the bugs, added them to the cookies and chocolate chips, and called the boys in for a feast. She watched as they ate every one.

Rebecca was entertaining and inspiring, but not, perhaps, an entirely reliable source of information. I'm sure she is better now, as a grown-up and an attorney. Most of my cousins, raised on the letter of the law, have become attorneys. I have grown up still researching Catholics, Hindus, Moslems, Buddhists, Republicans, and other people who were tantalizing mysteries in my North Carolina childhood. I'm working out my own beliefs now, and it's harder than I thought. I'm almost certain, though, that the thing about the frog and the plum tree is not right.

Biblical Family Values

I get confused when people talk about biblical family values. I wonder which biblical family they are talking about. Is it Abraham's family, where his wife Sarah persuaded him to sleep with her maid so the maid could bear him a child and then, when Sarah had her own son, convinced Abraham to throw out the maid and the boy into the desert with no food or water?

Or is it Jacob's family? He was tricked by his father-in-law into marrying his true love's sister instead of the woman he loved. Jacob then married the woman he loved in addition to her sister, and the two sisters had a baby-birthing competition that resulted in the twelve tribes of Israel.

Eleven of those children then sold their brother Joseph into slavery instead of murdering him, which was their original plan. They took his torn coat of many colors home after having soaked it in animal blood and told their father that his favorite son had been torn apart by wild animals. Put that family into modern times and you'd be talking years of therapeutic intervention at the very least. The biblical-family-values people would be shaking their heads, hearing about a family like that, and talking about the breakdown of society and blaming the women's movement.

When they say biblical family values, are they talking about King David's family? He fell in love with Bathsheba who was married to someone else. David had her husband sent to the front lines in battle. When he was killed, David married Bathsheba. Is that the family that embodies the values they're talking about?

Or is it David and Bathsheba's son Solomon that they are pointing to? He had seven hundred wives and three hundred concubines. Maybe I'm sticking to the Hebrew Bible too much. Let's look at Jesus' family. His mother was expecting before she was married, and Joseph raised Jesus even though he wasn't his flesh and blood. Those seem to be good values to me, but they aren't usually the ones preached by the family values crowd. Jesus himself certainly didn't grow up to be a conservative pillar of the community with a family of his own, a mini-van, and a job with regular hours. I don't think some of those people would approve of him much. Certainly they would never run him for office.

Biblical families are real, like ours and the ones next door. There are stepchildren and feuds, adultery and intrigue, anguish and love, caring, intimacy, violence, revenge. I can't see the biblical-family-values people wanting to know about actual biblical families. I can't see them wanting those families in their neighborhoods or their churches. Do they think we don't read the Bible for ourselves? Maybe they haven't read it. Maybe they hope we let them feed the Bible to us in simple pieces. Easy to chew up. Easy to digest. I heard a songwriter from Lubbock, Texas, summarize on public radio one of these bite-sized Bible bits. He said, "We learned two things: God loves you, and he'll send you straight to Hell, and sex is evil, dirty, and dangerous, and you should save it for the one you love."

The biblical families they are talking about are not the ones I spent so much time studying in seminary. The Radical Right can push whatever political agenda it wants to, and they can try to legislate whatever morality they want to. This is a democracy, and we are all free to push our values in the public arena. When they talk about biblical family values, though, be sure to ask them which biblical family lived out the upright sugary visions dancing in their heads. I'd be interested in the answer.

Procrastination

I have been putting off some writing I need to do. I procrastinate exceptionally well, so I thought I would share some of my techniques. First of all, music can clear the mind, so I listen to the radio for a while before I sit down at the computer. Who can work well with an overcrowded brain? A little music is just the thing to soothe the jangle of too many thoughts and projects milling around in a limited space. The minute I get ready to sit down, a song comes on the radio that demands a dance. Some songs do, you know. I dance, and my body warms up, which is good, because I work better with warm loose joints and muscles. After I dance I do some push-ups. I'm getting ready to take the second-degree black belt test at my karate school, and I have to be able to do a hundred push-ups and a hundred sit-ups. I need to practice often. When I'm through with exercising I take a shower, because it's not good to work when you're all sweaty.

When I get out of the shower, I notice my apartment needs some picking up so it will be as fresh and clean as I am. I put the dishes in the dishwasher and hang up the clothes that are on the floor. I put in a load of laundry. Who can work in the middle of a mess? I remember the Zen saying, "As without, so within." I know I'm doing a spiritual thing, creating an orderly environment.

It is good to create peace and order on the inside, too, so I decide to meditate for twenty minutes. I sit on the bed and count my breaths. Soon the mattress is pressing uncomfortably against the backs of my legs so I sit cross-legged for a while. That turns out not to be so comfortable, so I lie down. The last thought I remember is that a nap might be just the thing. I'll wake up refreshed and then tackle the writing with renewed creative energy.

When I wake up I make some coffee, return the phone calls that came in while I was asleep, then I sit down at the desk and turn on the computer. I close the blinds so I don't spend the whole afternoon looking out the window. I notice the cord on the blinds is crooked. I straighten it out. As I'm pulling up the computer file, I see that I have saved way too many files on the hard drive. I really should put them into file folders in the directories where they belong. Forty minutes later, everything is easy to find. I feel proud of myself. I have accomplished so much.

Music is playing and my mind is refreshed, my apartment is clean and I'm ready to write. On the radio comes Shawn Colvin singing "Killing the Blues." I have been wanting to learn that song for a long time. I grab a pen and get the words to the song written down. When I've got the words down, I pick up my guitar and work out the chords. Thirty minutes later I can play it pretty well. I've accomplished so much.

On my way back to the computer, I replace the smoke alarm that has been hanging down since last Thursday when I microwaved some popcorn. Finally I'm sitting at the computer, but I'm not working on my project. I'm describing my excellent techniques of procrastination. I'm accomplishing so much.

Prisoner of Cool

I had a crisis of coolness while standing in line at the post office. I was waiting to mail a package, minding my own business, when I heard a bird in the room. A big bird, tweeting and chirping, sounding like it was coming from the ceiling.

Here's where my mind started tripping over itself. If some human being were making that sound, it would be uncool to look around, craning my neck to see the birds in the ceiling. That person would be chirping to make me look for the bird, so they could be amused at how gullible and goofy I was.

On the other hand, I refuse to be a fearful person. I don't want to turn into someone who can stand in line right under a huge chirping bird and not even glance around for fear of looking like an idiot. That would make me a prisoner of cool.

I have known prisoners of cool. They can't have much fun. They don't let themselves laugh loudly in the movies; they can't be thrilled by a beautiful sight or delighted by an ordinary moment. They're always saying things like: "Take it easy . . ." or "You're easy to please . . ." when they deign to speak. Usually the ones I know just give sardonic looks from under a raised eyebrow, or they shake their heads with a secret smile.

A prisoner of cool would never crane her neck in the post office to look for a big bird. In making the decision to look or not to look, which took about ten seconds in actual post office time, I asked myself two questions: "What do you want to do?" and "What would the woman you want to become do?"

I want to become the kind of woman who has such amazing powers that she can know not only which of the people standing in line behind her was making a bird noise, but also the thoughts of each person there, along with what was in their hearts. I want to be able to sense the vibrations of whatever life forms were in the building and be able to communicate with them telepathically.

I didn't have the feeling that my amazing powers were going to kick in that day. Even if they never do, I want to become a great old person. You know how some old people seem to have a deep affection for the dailiness of life, and others are always dissatisfied and disappointed? I have a friend whose mother says every year, "This year's fall colors just aren't as brilliant as last year's." She has said that for the past twenty years. Are the leaves growing dull or are her senses?

I want to become an old woman who would crane her neck looking for the bird. So that's what I did. There wasn't a bird. The man behind the desk noticed me looking around and said in a bored voice, "That guy comes in here and does that all the time."

In back of me was a round man with slick black hair who looked energetically innocent. The bird-call man. He was good. I felt dumb, which annoyed me. What a geeky joke.

That's just my youth talking, though. The old woman I am going to become would throw her head back and laugh. She might compliment the man on his bird-call prowess. Maybe even ask for a lesson. Now that's a cool old lady.

Good Chemistry

My Aunt Dorothy was visiting three or four months ago from Nicaragua. While driving together through the mountains of Western North Carolina, she told me about her work at a high school in Massachusetts where James Taylor was a student. He had difficulty getting to chemistry class on time. Fifteen or twenty minutes into the class period, he would shamble in, and finally the chemistry teacher lost patience with him. Aunt Dorothy called him into her office for a serious talk.

"I said to him, 'James Taylor, you are going to have to find a way to get to chemistry class on time.'

"'I'm sorry, Mrs. Beuscher,' he said, hanging his head. 'I was up all night again writing a song.'

"'James,' I said, 'writing songs is nice, but you have the rest of your life to think about, and you have to understand, chemistry is very important.'" We threw back our heads and laughed. Life is funny.

Singing is his joy, and it's worked out pretty well for him. I love to sing, too, even though I'm no James Taylor. One of my lifelong dreams came true a couple of months ago. I got to sing in a bar in a neighboring town. The owners didn't exactly invite me to sing; they invited my friend, Joy, but I went over there on a slow night to listen to her, and Joy coaxed me to the microphone to sing a couple of numbers. It went to my head like a drug; I *have* to do it again.

What is it about singing that is so intimate, so satisfying? It can't be just the attention. You know how I know that? Because I saw Sylvester Stallone singing on the Muppet Show. I told a friend, and she said I must have been having a controlled substance flashback from my high school years, but I know what I saw.

Stallone was dressed like a bartender from the 1890s with a striped shirt, a vest, an arm band, and a derby hat. Miss Piggy was on his right, Kermit the frog on his left. You couldn't call it singing, really, he was talking the words. The puppets were singing.

Why would Stallone do that? He doesn't need the attention. He does so many other things well—he has big shiny muscles, he hangs from cliffs, he shoots big guns and collects expensive art and marries lingerie models. Yet he sings, or whatever you want to call it, on the Muppet Show.

There's something about singing that is magical. I saw Rudolph Nureyev on the Muppet Show, too. He danced with a huge furry monster, but after the commercial he came back and sang. It wasn't a total humiliation, but it did leave me puzzling over his reasons, and I think I've figured out part of it.

I think singing is religious. The word "religion" means "to reconnect." Something about singing reconnects you to your soul and to the One. Singing makes that even more powerful. The breath comes through you, the sound comes out of you, and your soul touches another person's soul. That is a religious experience. It is exciting and erotic. And if you haven't heard the words "erotic" and "religious" in the same paragraph before, stick with me.

Dancing at Long Meetings

I've sat in some long meetings in my time. Church meetings, faculty meetings, Women's Shelter meetings. I got so burned out at one point that if my presence wasn't crucial to the meeting and if not much was happening, I would wait until I'd been there an hour, look at my watch, gasp, and leave. The situation was desperate. If I hadn't jumped up and left, I might have started whooping loudly or singing or drumming on the table.

What if I had followed Kant's universal principle for ethical decision making and asked myself what would happen if everyone did what I had done? If everyone gasped and looked at her watch after an hour, there probably wouldn't be many meetings lasting more than an hour. That sounds good and sane.

I was at an all-day meeting about a month ago. I stayed all day, and it was a delight. Here's what we did. Decisions were based on consensus, so instead of voting, we planned to discuss something until we could all agree. Six roles were described that would be played during the meeting. Each of us volunteered to fill one role. The first was the Facilitator, the one who would keep us on track. Another was the Dissenter, who would play devil's advocate by presenting the negatives to each decision.

The role I took was Humorist for the day. Everyone at the table looked at me when the position was described, so I volunteered. My job was to make wisecracks, lighten up the atmosphere, and direct everyone to stop if the discussion got stuck. I could ask everyone to dance or play a game or paint each other's toenails—whatever I wanted. I wasn't sure how I felt about the job. Usually I do make cracks throughout a meeting because I'm acting out, I'm being obnoxious, I'm rebelling against the structure. They had made me part of the structure. How could I be a delinquent under such difficult circumstances?

I discovered that being humorous is more fun for me than being a delinquent. I had a good time instead of choosing to act out by not being funny. In the meeting we accomplished a lot, and we got to put on a Joan Osborne tape and turn it up loud and dance for a while to get the blood moving in our bodies partway through the long afternoon.

If I were to apply Kant's universal principle to this, I'd say if every meeting had some humor, conscience, and dancing in it, the world might be a better place. Can you picture it? Perhaps peace talks would go better if all parties danced a bit together. Maybe the President and Congress could crank up some Springsteen and blow it out one day. See what happens.

Wish You Hadn't Said That

People say cruel things to each other in the name of spirituality. My mother died of breast cancer nearly fifteen years ago. Toward the end, people would gather around her to pray. Before the praying started, a minister talked about how you had to really believe if you wanted prayer to work. If you had faith, the mountain would move. He said he had seen prayer efforts fail because one person in the room was an unbeliever. I knew I didn't believe hard enough that this prayer would save my mother. If I stayed in the room, the prayers for her healing might be damaged. So I left.

I'm angry about that now. I know that man was wrong. What kind of god would tell her children that they can ask for things, but if they don't believe hard enough, they will never get what they ask for? God made us with brains that think and doubt and question. If she made us this way, why would she punish us for it? I would never mock my children that way, and I know she's a better mother than I am.

I was leading a dream interpretation group one day when a woman told us the story of losing her twenty-three-year-old son to cancer. Another woman leaned across the table toward her and said, "Maybe it would be good if you could look at why he attracted that kind of suffering into his life, and what your soul might have needed that it attracted that suffering into your life."

I regret to say that I did not lunge over the table at that woman and throttle her. She was white, well-off, stunningly beautiful, and gifted. Of course that philosophy made sense to her.

She was one of those earnest people who say things like, "You create your own reality." I have one simple rule on pronouncements like that: "Don't say anything about suffering that you couldn't say in front of a hungry eleven-year-old girl in an African refugee camp." My rule sharply narrows the range of pronouncements I can make. It knocks "you create your own reality" right out of the running.

"You create your own reality" is a valuable saying for middle-class white people who blame their spouse for the state of their marriage, or claim their bosses don't like them as they lose job after job. In a slew of ways, we people who are moderately well off in America *do* create our own reality. As soon as you cross the border into the Third World, however, it would be good manners to fall silent.

I'm working on creating a reality for myself where earnest people and their earnest pronouncements don't annoy me so much. I'm building a reality with more patience, more mischief, more love, more adventure, a reality where I can ask Spirit for her intervention if one of my children is ill, knowing that she loves my doubts as much as my certainties. I want to create a reality where I can answer an earnest pronouncement like "you create your own reality" with compassion instead of hostility. Y'all pray for my healing—even if you don't believe it'll do any good.

Smile Big and No One Will Notice

My mother's name was Katherine Pressly Hamilton. She grew up in India because her parents were missionaries to the Hindus and Muslims who used to live in and around the town of Lahore, which is now in Pakistan. I remember her standing at the sink washing dishes while singing hymns in Urdu. One year I invited a Pakistani student home for Thanksgiving dinner. He cried when she spoke to him in Urdu. He said she had such a village accent, it made him terribly homesick. The Ethiopian man from Moscow I had also invited converted to capitalism while playing Monopoly after dinner, but that's another story.

Mama and her sister and brothers would cook curry when they got together. Mabel, the oldest, wanted it mild. Her brother Lindsay would wait until her back was turned to uncap the curry and pour in the rest of the bottle. When they were children, they would come from India on the boat for furlough. Their father would preach in Carolina churches and the children would sing in Hindi and put on little skits as part of the program. The kids would change the words of some of the songs to say things like: "Please pass me the beer." It would have shocked their parents terribly, and there would have been hell to pay, but they got away with it because their parents' command of the language was still shaky.

Mama said their American aunts would cry when her family got off the boat. One of them finally told her after she was grown that it was because the children looked so piti-ful in their missionary barrel clothes. She didn't know the clothes were ten years out of date. She didn't know that most people wouldn't wear clothes that had tiny tears or stains. When I was a girl and something I wanted to wear had a little spot on the front or had a safety pin holding up the hem, she would always say, "Just throw back your shoul-ders, smile big, and no one will notice."

Mama was a believer in smiling. She preferred to stay happy. Part of her technique for staying happy was to see things in the most positive way. "The days I gave birth to you girls were the happiest of my life. Every minute of it was won-derful. Wonderful." I am grown now, and I have given birth. Those days were wonderful, but "every minute"? I think she must have had some powerful drugs.

"Willfully positive" is how I would describe my mother's style, even about her marriage. She and my father didn't live together from the time I was three, but they stayed married. She used to say, "Your father is a difficult man, but I love him." Once I read a survey she had filled out in a *Reader's Digest* left lying on the bathroom floor. One question asked, "If you had to do it over again, would you get married?" She had checked "No." I was shocked.

My father used to come for supper at our house every night and stayed the evening before going home to his apartment in town. Children get used to their family's ways. If I had ever given their marriage much thought, I wouldn't have been shocked. I didn't have to give it much thought because most days my mother threw her shoulders back and smiled. We all did.

The main challenge for me today is not letting my smile hide me from reality. There is a temptation not to think about things I don't want to think about. One of the lessons I learned from my Mama was to lie to myself. I am trying to unlearn it. Can I be positive and honest, too? Can I smile big and still be aware that there is a rip in my hem or a tear on my cheek? I'm going to struggle with that. But I'll be smiling, so you probably won't notice.

A Time for Darkness

In the bleak midwinter frosty wind made moan, earth stood hard as iron, water like stone. Snow had fallen, snow on snow, snow on snow, in the bleak midwinter long ago."

This is the season when dark is growing strong, reaching its peak at the winter solstice on December 21. On December 22, the earth begins tilting the Northern Hemisphere gradually back toward our sun. The light begins to grow stronger, and every culture in the Northern Hemisphere celebrates the rebirth of the light. Hindus have Divali, Jews have Hannukah, Pagans have Yule, Christians have Christmas.

Jesus was probably born in spring, since the story says shepherds were out in the fields at night, and it is usually too cold for that in Bethlehem at the end of December. The Christian Church set the date of Jesus' birth celebration to coincide with a huge celebration in the Roman Empire that was already taking place on December 25. That way the birth of the Son could be celebrated at the same time as the birth of the Sun. Both are symbols of the birth of The Light in the hearts and minds of human beings.

For some of us, The Light as a symbol can represent the light of reason, by which we find our way in life. We honor reason in our tradition, and rebel against any faith system that demands we put aside our need for things to make sense. For others, The Light can represent the light of Spirit that ebbs and flows inside us as we feel sometimes drained and dusty, and other times energetic, enthusiastic, and supple. Some times in our lives are spirited times and others are dispirited times. As we contemplate the meanings of the dark times and the light times, the earth-based traditions would caution us against using The Dark as a symbol for all that is negative. If we use "darkness" to speak about ignorance, depression, and evil, we speak as if it would be best to have no darkness at all, to have light all the time. That would be awful. There is a season for dark and a season for light.

Is it possible then that there is a time to feel energetic and a time to feel drained in the rhythm of life? A time to let life and energy flow outward from you, and a time for it to flow inward? Maybe the ebb and flow of Spirit is a rhythm that is good to feel. Maybe in our growing into wholeness there is a time to feel dusty and dry, "hard as iron" like the winter ground, and stony as winter water. Maybe instead of worrying and suffering over those feelings we could settle into them, knowing that there is a time for cold and a time for warmth, a time to be energetic and a time to rest, a time to grow and a time to stay where you are, a time for the light of reason and a time for other ways of knowing. Maybe we could walk in beauty and balance more easily if we could welcome the dark time, trusting that when it reaches its full strength, things will begin their tilt back in the other direction. Nothing stays the same in the flow of things. All things seek their balance and their rhythm. The wheel will always turn. The light will always be reborn. We need not be afraid. This month, as humans have done for thousands of years, we can bid goodbye to The Dark in peace and greet the rebirth of The Light with rejoicing.

We Three Kings and Fourteen Schizophrenics

All I can say is you haven't lived until you've sung "We Three Kings" with fourteen paranoid schizophrenics on Christmas Eve.

At seven o'clock the Christmas Eve I was fifteen, my father developed an urgent need to go caroling. He loved the idea of serving humanity, but the actuality of serving humanity was too time-consuming, too much trouble, and too little applauded for any of us to have done much of it. Christmas is a time, though, when one's thoughts turn to helping others. You watch "A Christmas Carol" and "It's a Wonderful Life" and you feel moved to do something loving and giving.

My dad had not yet done any Christmas service to humanity, and since it was Christmas Eve, the deadline was fast approaching. We hadn't even bought our Christmas tree, but my dad had an impulse to go caroling, and he wanted me and my thirteen-year-old sister to go with him.

We wailed that it would be terminally embarrassing to go caroling with him around our neighborhood. The neighborhood, he informed us cheerfully, was not what he had in mind. He felt called to go caroling eight miles down the road—at the Norristown State Mental Hospital.

If you have ever known a teenage girl, you know my sister and I had sulking, sighing, and rolling our eyes raised to an art form. My dad, though, was an artist himself: at growling, jollying, guilting, and flashing a charismatic personality. By seven-thirty we were slumped in the back seat of the blue Olds. My twelve-string guitar was riding in the trunk. By seven forty-five we pulled up to the heavy wrought-iron gates of the mental hospital.

My dad had called ahead and spoken to someone in the office, but that person had not told the guards at the gate. At first they looked at us with suspicion, but my father was famous in Philadelphia at that time because he was on the 6 and 11 o'clock TV news. They had seen his face before. In five minutes they had been charmed into believing we weren't there to break out an insane serial killer, so they let us in and gave us directions to the building where they thought we might want to sing.

The staff people in that building were surprised to see us, too, but they were kind. With good grace they began directing patients to the lobby where we three carolers stood. The staff set up chairs while we waited.

I was completely humiliated. I let my hair hang in front of my face and pretended to be invisible. My little sister copied me, naturally. The patients started shuffling in, holding their heads at a too-far-back angle that I now know meant heavy doses of Thorazine. In their dishwater gray hospital gowns it was hard to tell anyone's age. Everybody looked old, even the young ones. They shuffled to their chairs. My dad motioned for me to get out my guitar.

We started with "The First Noel" and "Hark! The Herald Angels Sing." A woman wearing bright red lipstick on her lips, her cheekbones, and in a circle on her chin, slapped her legs and sang loudly in time with the music. Her voice sounded like something between a crow and a warning siren, and she didn't bother with words. She especially liked "Joyful, Joyful, We Adore Thee." We started smiling at each other. Her enjoyment became a blaze that caught in the rest of us. One by one, each of the patients joined us in singing. It was during "We Three Kings" that I forgot to act cool. We were having Christmas, and the whole dark place, just for a moment, was lit with joy.

Sick and Surly

When I feel myself coming down with something I start emergency measures. I quit staying up late. I eat vitamins in just the right amount at just the right times. I drink eight glasses of water a day. I don't stop eating cheeseburgers, though. I've got to save something for when I am in serious trouble.

Mark Twain told the story of a virtuous man who died because he had no vices to give up. He fell sick and his doctor told him he had to give up alcohol to get better. "But, Doctor," he said, "I don't drink alcohol."

"Give up smoking, then."

"But, Doctor, I don't smoke!"

"Quit staying up all night at parties with wild women, then."

The sick man never did that either, and, having no vices to give up, he died. I'm keeping cheeseburgers in reserve.

For the run-of-the-mill kinds of sicknesses, I go to bed early, eat vitamins, drink water, and sip hot lemonade with honey. My mother used that remedy for just about everything.

It makes me mad to be sick. Somewhere I got the idea that sickness shouldn't happen. I don't plan for it in my world. I feel that my body should go on sturdily working like my '88 Accord, not making a fuss, never asking for too much attention.

In my family while I was growing up, we didn't mollycoddle our bodies. If you were really sick, you went to the hospital. If you weren't in the hospital you weren't really sick. Once my head hurt and my mother said, "Children don't get headaches." So I didn't get them anymore. At least, I didn't let myself acknowledge or even feel them. Allergies were more suspect than headaches. Adults would speak of it by deepening their voice and rolling their eyes: "Oh, you know, her son has—allergies." Imagine my surprise, a month after the birth of my first child, when I began itching all over my neck after patting the cat we'd had for the past six years. I had a vague feeling that something was morally wrong with me for having this allergy, so I felt itchy and guilty at the same time.

This past year I have been sick a lot. Not sick enough to go to the hospital, just sick enough to lie on the sofa looking pale and heroic. I don't know why I have been sick so much. I think it must be the karma fairy.

I have matured in compassion because the karma fairy has visited on me every single thing I used to look down on other people for having. You meet the karma fairy when, right after you curse righteously at someone who has cut in front of your car, you cut off someone else within the hour. You didn't see the other driver. It must be his fault. Your sneaking suspicion, though, is that you just did the very thing for which you were pouring contempt on someone else.

Now that the karma fairy has taught me about being sick, I'm more compassionate toward other people. Not to myself, though. I still get mad: *What*? I have to rest? I *hate* to rest. I might have to cancel appointments? Say it ain't so.

Someone may have to bring me hot lemonade and honey and pat my face and kiss my pale cheek? Well, okay. Just don't make me give up cheeseburgers.

Subversive Behavior

When I was teaching a class called "Women in Religion," I gave my students an assignment. For the duration of the class we were going to talk about God as "she" and "Mother" instead of "he" and "Father." I know it's ridiculous to call God "she," as if God were female. But it's equally ridiculous to call God "he," as if God were male. Since the Judeo-Christian culture has been calling God "he" for the last four thousand years, I told my students, perhaps one semester of calling God "she" will begin to balance that a bit. Every semester their reactions were explosive. One young woman said angrily, "I could *never* call on a mother God if I really needed help. She wouldn't have the power to do anything." What does that say about her sense of her own mother? About her sense of herself as a female?

Another student had gone out to dinner with her parents and was telling them about our class and about having to call God "Mother." A waitress hovered behind them, wiping a table for long minutes and listening. When they got up to leave, she came over to my student and said, "Honey, you better quit calling God 'Mother' because if you don't, you're goin' straight to hell."

I usually keep my efforts at education confined to the classroom, but not always. I was scheduled to speak to a women's group at a small country church several years ago, and when I arrived nothing was ready, no one was gathered. I'm not even sure the minister had told anyone I was coming. I was left on my own in the Sunday school wing of the building while they got themselves organized. I wandered into the nursery and then into what looked like a primary grade classroom. There were crayons and blunt scissors, scraps of colored paper on low tables. On a bulletin board, I saw a picture in crayon on pink construction paper of a man with wings, a halo, a long brown beard, and a serious expression. The caption, in large capital letters, read "GOD."

What else could I do? I looked around for more construction paper and, with a crayon, I drew a picture of a woman with a smile, gray curly hair, and big breasts. I gave her wings and a halo and wrote in big letters the caption: "GOD."

When people hear about the Supreme Being as being only male, they get unbalanced. If God is male, then males are closer to what God is like than females. Men might start to feel like they are supposed to know everything and be able to control everything, like they can't stop and ask for directions when they need to. How exhausting.

Women might start to feel like their bodies and spirits are less sacred than men's, like their ways of doing things are wrong or stupid and that God doesn't care much about birthing or bleeding or feeding a child from their body. They might start to doubt whether they know anything or can control anything. That's exhausting, too.

As a therapist, I have seen the results of this exhaustion and imbalance. That's why I do my little part to drive people nuts. Because where people are going nuts, you know something important is going on.

Traditional Marriage

I'm a bit confused. In Spartanburg there are large billboards that say, "Our community supports traditional marriage." Well, yeah. I'm trying to think of ways to support traditional marriage. Then I get to thinking, what *is* a traditional marriage? Maybe I think too much. A traditional marriage. How far back are we going for these traditions? Because if we go back to biblical times, we have the traditional marriage of Abraham where he and his wife traveled quite a bit. A couple of times when Abraham was in fear of his life he lied and said his wife was his sister, so the Pharaoh took her for one of his concubines. Then when the Pharaoh found out, he threw them both out of the country for violating *his* traditional morals, which dictated you don't do things like that.

Or are we talking about the traditional marriage of Isaac where his father sent a servant to pick out a wife for him, and the servant brought her back to Isaac who took her into his tent and made her his wife? Or their son Jacob's marriage, where he worked seven years for Rachel and then was given her older sister in a sneaky way after he had drunk enough at the wedding feast not to know the difference until it was too late? Then he married Rachel, too.

Are we talking about traditional marriages where the parents decide who their children are going to marry? Are we talking about traditional American marriages? American marriages from the 1600s? The Victorian Era, where women were not allowed to have anesthesia during childbirth, not allowed to own property, not even legally considered to have custody of their children?

Just how far back into history are we supposed to go? Back to the last century when there was no birth control information to be had? When it was not illegal for a man to beat his wife or rape her? No wait, that wasn't the last century. In South Carolina, that was the early eighties. I'd be willing to talk about supporting traditional marriage if people would have the manners to tell me what it is they want me to support.

Someone told me that traditional marriage means marriage between a man and a woman, but I said that couldn't be it. Why would marriage between a man and a woman need any more support than it already has? It's the only kind of marriage that's legal. It's the kind of marriage almost everyone has. It's the kind you see on TV and the only kind little kids are taught about in school and the only kind that is mentioned in books and the only kind you see pictures of in magazines. How much more support than that do they want?

If marriage between a man and a woman is the one they want us to support, that would mean they were against same-gendered people joining together in commitment. That can't be it. The Christian Right is *for* marriage, right? They support commitment between two people. It is what makes our society stable. Gay people being able to marry wouldn't threaten marriages between men and women. I mean, it's not as if legalizing same-sex marriage would suddenly make men all over the place say, "Oh, golly, I *was* going to marry a woman, but now I think I'll marry a man." Or women saying, "You know, I had been dreaming of marrying a man, but now that it's legal to marry my best friend, I think I'll do that!" On second thought, that last one sounds pretty good. Marrying my best friend. Hmmm. I must think about those billboards some more.

Going to an Inner Party

I don't know if you have this experience, but I find overheard conversations are more interesting than the ones I'm part of. Television sounds more interesting if I don't catch exactly what's being said; an unopened Christmas present is always better than an opened one; the inventions I think up while half asleep are more fabulous than the ones my waking mind comes up with; and what's about to happen is more interesting than what's happening now. The thoughts along the edges of the mainstream are more interesting than the ones in full consciousness.

I don't know what to call it when mis-reading and mis-hearing things are a source of inspiration and delight. Right now I think of it as my inner poet. I picture her as a tricky laughing woman who's cross-eyed from trying to see around corners.

Here's what I'm talking about: I heard someone on the radio say faintly, "It's coming in at the speed of snow." I still don't know what they really said, but who cares? "It's coming in at the speed of snow" is something you'd hear in a dream. What exactly is the speed of snow? It's a Zen koan. The imagination opens and the linear train of thought derails.

Rereading something I had written the other day, I found a typo. I was talking about a dinner party and I had left off the "d." Going to an "inner party" sounds fun, although I'm not sure how you'd get there, who would be invited, and what would be served. I'm pretty sure you'd get to dance, though, and I think once in a while I've heard the music.

Driving home from the mountains one afternoon, I saw a sign for the Trinity Fish Camp. When I looked again it said Tri-city Fish Camp, but I think "trinity" is a better name. After all, Jesus was a fisherman, and because one member of the trinity spent a lot of time fishing, I think it's an apt name. You can picture the disciples at the Trinity Fish Camp, sitting around a paper-covered table cracking crabs and talking theology, hush-puppy crumbs in their beards.

Another time I thought I saw a sign that said Children's Truck Stop, and I got to thinking what a children's truck stop might be like. Would children bring their trucks, gas them up, get the windshields washed? Would they buy tiny boots and eat small burgers with pecan swirls for dessert? I know there would be video games.

I love the flickering things that bump along the edges of mainstream consciousness. These glimpses of an inner wisdom flash like fish in a creek, and if I can grab one by the tail I feel like I have a treasure. I'll keep fishing for them, and I'll share them with you. But right now I've got to go. I'm off to an inner party at the speed of snow.

Fireworks at the Wedding

I dreamed one night that fireworks had exploded and blown a big hole in the church where I grew up. Fireworks and church may not seem to go together, but in my family they do.

In the North Carolina branch of my mother's family, we have fireworks at every major celebration: the Fourth of July, New Year's, Thanksgiving, Christmas, birthdays, the first and last days of school, and weddings. Especially weddings. This is in all other ways a dignified and conservative family, filled with doctors and ministers, teachers, lawyers, and missionaries. It was my missionary grandfather who brought the custom back from India where fireworks enliven the best festivities. Several of the dignified pillars of the family disapprove of fireworks at weddings, so we have to sneak to set them off. Fireworks aren't the only mischief in the family, but they are the central mischief.

At a recent family wedding, I heard one of my cousins talking to his two-year-old nephew. "Darlin'," he said, "there is going to be a beautiful lady in that church carrying some flowers. Now, son, some of those flowers are for you. So when she walks by, you just run up and grab you a handful . . ."

As the service began, one cousin slipped outside. No one noticed. We practice not noticing; it's part of the protocol. A few minutes later, when my opera singer cousin was hit-ting the high notes in "Where Sheep May Safely Graze," we heard the cannon fire. Then, from right outside the open windows came the rapid-fire volleys of the Black Cats that come in strings of twenty or thirty firecrackers. It made an ungodly racket. The entire crowd on the groom's side of the church jumped in their seats and looked around, wild-eyed. The cellist in the string quartet fell off her chair. On the bride's side, my family gazed calmly straight ahead, squinting a little against the acrid smoke that drifted through the windows into the sanctuary. No one giggled. That is against the code. No one even smiled.

At one family wedding, the minister was told by the mother of the bride about our tradition of fireworks. She did not want any fireworks at this wedding. Like we say here in the South, that minister had a fit and fell in it. He instructed the rehearsal party on the sacredness of the occasion, a sacredness that was not to be sullied by fun or high spirits. To drive his point home, he told the Old Testament story about two people who touched the Ark of the Covenant without permission. They were struck dead for sullying a sacred thing. The wedding party stared at their shoes. This wasn't covered in our family wedding protocol.

At this wedding, guards were hired and posted outside the church building. One string of Black Cats did get lit, but we only heard three pops.Those strings are hard to stop once they get started. I imagine one of the guards threw himself bodily on it. There was a brief incident at the reception where an uncle set off his cannon and his sister, the mother of the bride, called the police. They came and investigated. There was a lot of talking into police radios, but, in Kings Mountain, North Carolina, the police just don't arrest orthopedic surgeons in the middle of the day, even if they shoot off a fireworks cannon in a residential area.

My dream was telling me a truth. Fireworks did blow a hole in that childhood church of mine. Each explosion let in a little fresh air. They supply a welcome balance to the self-sacrifice and stern structure that is so much a part of that religious tradition. I left that church long ago for a freer and more liberal one, but I honor joy and celebration in any religion. I'm glad to have been taught that the sacred and the silly walk well hand in hand.

Rock of Ages at the Taj Mahal

In July of 1985 I was on a bus in the middle of India with forty Muslims, Hindus, Jews, Christians, Buddhists, and Moonies. We were touring the world for two months to study each others' religions.

We were on our way to the Taj Mahal, four hours from our hotel in New Delhi. The bus was painted turquoise to ward off evil spirits and hung all over with garlands of marigolds. The day was hot; the road was dusty and full of holes. I was sitting next to Gary from Alabama, who had been raised Southern Baptist but was now a Moonie, and we talked as the bus bumped and jolted us down the road.

I love talking to people who are on the fringes of my religious experience. Hearing about exotic beliefs and strange practices is one of my favorite hobbies. The Moonies certainly seemed out there on the fringe to me, so I had been pestering them to tell me what they believed. We had a good time questioning each other, sometimes debating, often laughing. Gary and I had gotten to be friends. One of the things we all did to pass the time on long bus rides was to look through each other's wallets, perusing pictures of loved ones, mocking driver's license photos, flipping through insurance cards, love notes, and bank receipts.

Another thing we did to pass the time on long bus and plane rides was to tell what we'd be doing this day and this hour if we were home. It was a Saturday, and I was telling Gary that my husband and I would be getting ready to go over to our friends' house for supper. We would grill chicken, eat vegetables with spinach dip, and sit in the dining room under the black velvet painting of Elvis. The painting had been an anniversary gift from us, and they would hang it up on Saturday nights when we came over. After supper we would move to the living room and sing hymns around the piano, starting with the Navy Hymn about "those in peril on the sea," working up to what we called "blood hymns." Blood hymns were the old timey ones about the blood of Jesus, the ones with the questionable theology and stirring tunes that so many of us secretly love.

Gary said, "I know about blood hymns—I grew up Southern Baptist!" We started singing. We harmonized on "There's Power in the Blood" and "There is a Fountain Filled With Blood" and "Are You Washed in the Blood?" We had a fine time, and we got applause from the Sikhs who were sitting behind us with their long beards, white turbans, and curved daggers on their belts. They sang us some Sikh songs and we applauded. Then the Buddhist monks from Nepal sitting across the aisle were moved to chant, and the sound of their voices resonated through the turquoise bus, making our breastbones vibrate. That hot afternoon for hours we heard Russian Orthodox hymns, songs from Finland, Rasta gospel from Jamaica, and a spell for making yourself impervious to fire from a witch doctor named André who lives in Surinam with his ten beautiful wives and forty-seven children.

These days, when I hear about the peaceable kingdom where the lion will lie down with the lamb, when I read about the clamor of nations struggling toward peace, I think about that day we sang our spirituals for each other, the day when Christ and Shiva clapped for each other and sang in harmony on a dusty road in a turquoise bus hung with marigolds.

Unitarian Universalist Meditation Manuals

This list includes all meditation manuals since the merger in 1961. For information about meditations prior to 1961, contact Skinner House Books, 25 Beacon Street, Boston, MA 02108.

1999 *The Rock of Ages at the Taj Mahal* Meg Barnhouse

Morning Watch Barbara Pescan

1998 *Glory, Hallelujah! Now Please Pick Up Your Socks* Jane Ellen Mauldin

Evening Tide Elizabeth Tarbox

1997 *A Temporary State of Grace* David S. Blanchard

Green Mountain Spring and Other Leaps of Faith Gary A. Kowalski

1996 *Taking Pictures of God* Bruce T. Marshall

Blessing the Bread Lynn Ungar

1995 *In the Holy Quiet of This Hour* Richard S. Gilbert

1994 *In the Simple Morning Light* Barbara Rohde

1993 *Life Tides* Elizabeth Tarbox

The Gospel of Universalism Tom Owen-Towle

1992 *Noisy Stones* Robert R. Walsh

1991 *Been in the Storm So Long* Mark Morrison-Reed and Jacqui James, Editors

1990 *Into the Wilderness* Sara Moores Campbell

1989 *A Small Heaven* Jane Ranney Rzepka

1988 *The Numbering of Our Days* Anthony Friess Perrino

1987 *Exaltation* David B. Parke, Editor

1986 *Quest* Kathy Fuson Hurt

1985 *The Gift of the Ordinary* Charles S. Stephen, Jr., Editor

1984 *To Meet the Asking Years* Gordon B. McKeeman, Editor

1983 *Tree and Jubilee* Greta W. Crosby

1981 *Outstretched Wings of the Spirit* Donald S. Harrington

1980 *Longing of the Heart* Paul N. Carnes

1979 *Portraits from the Cross* David Rankin

1978 *Songs of Simple Thanksgiving* Kenneth L. Patton

1977 *The Promise of Spring* Clinton Lee Scott

1976 *The Strangeness of This Business* Clarke D. Wells

1975 *In Unbroken Line* Chris Raible, Editor

1974 *Stopping Places* Mary Lou Thompson

1973 *The Tides of Spring* Charles W. Grady

1972 *73 Voices* Chris Raible and Ed Darling, Editors

1971 *Bhakti, Santi, Love, Peace* Jacob Trapp

1970 *Beginning Now* J. Donald Johnston

1969 *Answers in the Wind* Charles W. McGehee

1968 *The Trying Out* Richard Kellaway

1967 *Moments of Springtime* Rudolf Nemser

1966 *Across the Abyss* Walter D. Kring

1965 *The Sound of Silence* Raymond Baughan

1964 *Impassioned Clay* Ralph Helverson

1963 *Seasons of the Soul* Robert T. Weston

1962 *The Uncarven Image* Phillip Hewett

1961 *Parts and Proportions* Arthur Graham